Discarded, abando...
men and women are a...
purpose and grace ca...
miracle!

Bishop Patrick M. Schatzline

As a Pastor I have witnessed many things, but nothing prepared my heart for impact that some young men and women on the other side of the world had on me, my family and my church. As they shared the miraculous story of how the love of God through a man and his family found them in utter despair, lonely, abandoned, hungry and worst of all no hope! This book compiled by Dasa is a testament to what God's grace can do in a life that no one else found value in. You will I am sure shed tears as you read the saga of their lives, but I promise you, when you close this book you will have a smile in your heart of thanksgiving for our merciful heavenly father who can make "something "beautiful" of their lives.

Reverend Tony McAfee

I hope as you read this book you will get just a glimmer of what a remarkable group of young men and women God has assembled together in Moldova for His purposes. The stories of these "orphan kids" will make you cry tears of sadness and tears of joy just as I did when I met many of them on my first visit to Moldova. God used my time there to open my heart and in particular He used one amazing young women, Dasa, to touch my heart and show me God's love in action. Her faith and the faith of all these kids is genuine and serves as an example to each of us as they minister to those who are "the least among us." God is at work in Moldova through these "orphan kids" who are changing the world around them.

David Byrnes Founder/CEO, FACTS

Management Co,

President/Cofounder, Cape Kid Meals

Out of the Ashes

Our Story of Abandonment, Rejection, and Redemption

Compiled by Dasa Rosca

Out of the Ashes, Our Story of Abandonment,
Rejection, and Redemption
Compiled by Dasa Rosca

Published by The Orphans Hands
P.O. Box 242248
Montgomery, Alabama 36124
(334) 866-0069
www.theorphanshands.org

ISBN Paperback: 978-0-692593-56-1
Printed in the United States

Dedication

To all those born in the ruins of life, those that have felt the pain of rejection, abandonment and loneliness. To those that have been looked down at as worthless beings destined for failure. To those that have once been paralyzed with doubt, fear and sorrow. To all of you that chose to not let your past define you and instead walked the miraculous journey of redemption to reach His purpose for your life. Today you bring healing to the wounded, hope to the hopeless by touching a broken life with your love.

Acknowledgements

To the Cameron family. You have rescued us from the pit of darkness, you have picked us up and dusted us of all our pain and sorrow with your love. Thank you for seeing us worthy enough to open your home and your heart so those like us would know what belonging feels like.

Thank you.

Table of Contents

Out of the Ashes

Introduction

Twenty-five years ago I stared into the face of a little boy. It was winter outside and inside. The tepid radiators could not compete against the bitter cold that pressed against the solid concrete walls of the communist-style building.

I'd seen black and white films of concentration camps where dying kids stared blankly at the camera. This was live, in color, and with a raw foul smell. Hitler wasn't the reason for this injustice. Ceausescu, the recently assassinated dictator of Romania was. His communist-driven dictatorship made the lives of those under him unbearable. At the very bottom of this calamity, were these helpless waifs - the orphans.

This little boy was in the bitter cold and half naked. His own waste covered his starving body. His tummy was distended like pictures of Somali or Biafran children I'd seen. All around his scalp was raw; his hair was matted with only God knew what. The mattress in his crib was stained by years of waste. Patchy paint covered rusty bars. I found out later it was lead paint. The orphanage was eerily quiet. After the children cry and cry and no one comes, they give up.

The loudest sound was the clack-clack of metal cribs colliding as the filthy, hungry, lonely, children rocked back-and-forth trying to bring comfort to their hurting hearts. Loneliness is a terrible nurse.

I picked the little waif up; I knew he wasn't used to being held. His little back was stiff. He looked with curious mistrust at my face. He rubbed his raw skin I guess trying to tell me of his pain. I fumbled in my coat pocket and found a Mars chocolate bar. We sat on a chair and as I opened it he was pulling it from my hands. In seconds, it was gone. My sister Wendy walked past and reached towards me with a red apple. His little hands grabbed it all and without stopping, ate every bit until the seed pod fell on the ground. I had to hold him back from picking it off the filthy floor and putting it in his mouth. That is how I found Andrew. I promised the orphan in my arms that day that I'd be back. Every six weeks, till the day he was ours, I did come back.

What a day! Chrissie had never seen him. I looked through building that had become so familiar. Chrissie followed me up and down the stairs. A blanket lay on the floor with coffee and paint cans that were used for potties. They were left to sit on them for hours at a time that resulted in a raw circle on their bottoms. They were beaten if they moved off the blanket. It was torture. He wasn't in his own room. My heart sank. I'd come all the way from home to show Chrissie her son for the first time and he was gone. Every room on the bottom of the building was empty.

We went outside where there was the noise of little voices. We half ran to the fence and sitting on a blanket, just like the one inside - like a litter of puppies, huddled together - he was there.

I ran to him, picked him up, and carried him towards where Chrissie was standing. "This is him, this is Andrei," I said. I stretched my arms towards her and saw the very picture of God in my Chrissie's face.

He was wearing a cap. As she held him to her breast and slowly removed his hat so she could look at his little face. As the cap slid off his head, I saw that he had been shaved and was totally bald. I saw it; Chrissie didn't. Her eyes had a look in them I had never seen. She was drinking the visage of this four-year-old boy whom someone else had discarded. I stood transfixed watching her as she examined his ears and cheeks and rubbing her hands over his head - almost wiping away the four years he'd had in despair. In a few seconds, the orphan had become a son.

I didn't know it then, but my life had changed forever. He was the first to break our hearts as God's heart breaks for the lost. I thank God he hasn't been the last one.

We've found them in every situation - on sunny days and in winter rains. But, to our amazement, many of the young men and women that are also ours -not of blood but of spirit - have grown, like Andrew, out of the ashes into the miracle of heaven.

These orphans are The Orphan's Hands and now the hands that carry the message of Hope to the next generation of the lost.

We call her Dasa. Her given name is Feodosia, but do not call her that. I saw her first sitting on a park bench along with seventeen other girls. We had just replaced 391 windows in the largest orphanage in

Moldova. I was there with Chrissie to inspect the work and pay the final payment.

The director of the orphanage waved his arm towards the young girls saying, "They all must go."

I'd just built a house for girls who were at the risk of being trafficked. The house was already full. I turned to Chrissie, "how many beds can we put in the classroom?" Her eyes closed and counted, imagining where beds would fit in the small space. Three - only three. I looked back at the faces who had no idea the enormity of what was being decided just a few feet from where they sat. "Help me, please," I said to one of our girls that we'd taken from the orphanage to the new house. They knew what was about to happen and began to cry. "No dad, we can't." I turned again to the faces. Three girls were chosen that day: Dasa (who wrote this book), Nadea (Dasa's cousin who is the leader of the young men and women of the Orphans Hands in Moldova), and Natalie (who married my son three years ago, my orphan son chose her again, to be his wife).

Dasa was the most broken kid I'd met. She cried at any moment. She would hide behind doors or lie with her face against the wall, hiding from a life she'd long learned to hate. I couldn't reach her. I knew she was getting most of what I said because the language barrier was being torn down, but her heart was hidden deep within walls of hurt and rejection. I couldn't figure her out. One day it hit me. She had been conceived out of a one-night stand. The birth father had said, "if it's a boy I will keep it, if it's a girl I don't want her." She ended up in the orphanage. Every day Dasa dressed like a boy; hoping her dad would look over the orphanage wall and change his mind. He never came, not even once. She had suffered the worst thing of all, rejection. I looked at her blue eyes and began. This was my best last chance to reach her. I joked "I don't like boys, I love girls, will you be my daughter?" Her eyes filled with tears, she ran and hugged me. She was home. At the time of this book's publication, she is a student at Auburn University at Montgomery. She is on the Dean's List, and is an integral part of the ministry, both here and in Moldova.

Out of The Ashes

This book is dangerous. It will show you the orphans - not as a mass of humanity, but as real, dreaming, living souls -who are waiting for someone to come and make them blossom.

Philip Cameron

Out of the Ashes

Dasa

My official name is Feodosia Rosca and the name I now go by is Dasa Cameron.

When I was born, my father decided that he wanted nothing to do with me or my mother. Two years later, my mother left me with my uncle and went to Russia to look for a job. My mother only visited me twice a year. I remember having everything - food, toys, clothes, candies - but I wasn't happy. I wanted her in my life. Not a single day went by when I wasn't reminded by my auntie that I will end up like my mother, an embarrassment to the family. Sometimes I begged my uncle to take me back to the place where my mom and I had lived before. When I was five years old, he took me back and today, even though 19 years have passed, I still cry remembering this moment. Everything is still so real in my mind, like it happened yesterday, that lonely feeling, when I walked into our house trying to keep my tears back. I could smell my mom's perfume everywhere in the house. I used to hide in my mother's wardrobe, hug her clothes and fall asleep with tears running down my face and my heart broken from missing her so much.

My mother continued working abroad and over the next few years, I was left in the care of many people - passed on from one to another - some worse than the others. All I remember is their cruel words that beat me down every single time I heard them and the feeling that I was nothing but an inconvenience for my mother and everyone around me.

When I was nine-years-old, we moved to Russia. Life did not change that much because I did not get to see my mother for days at times, but I was happy because at least she did not leave me behind again. With time, things got better, life got a little easier and I had hope for a better future.

A few months later, my mother was in a car accident and almost lost her life. She was in a coma for fifteen days. It was then that I learned that life can take a different course in a matter of seconds.

My mother was never the same after the accident. She was mentally and physically changed forever. Being out of a job, we left everything we had behind and returned to Moldova. The adjustment was not easy and I learned another lesson: just because a door is closed that we are convinced will never open again, does not mean that the door will stay forever closed. Rather, it will often become the only exit door out of a situation. I had to go back to the same school, the same old life, the same old pain in my heart. It wasn't easy. Sometimes I came home from school and there was no food on the table. Winters were cold and the glimmer of hope I tasted in Russia was long gone.

A few years later, my mother returned to Russia leaving me in the care of my uncle again. My uncle's family made a decision believing it was the best choice for me and sent me to the orphanage.

The orphanage was not the best place to be, but it taught me how to survive. I was lonely. I was angry. I felt unwanted and unloved. The memories with my mother was all I had, and I held on to them dearly. I had no dreams. I believed that an orphan is not allowed to dream or hope.

When I was 16 years old, the day I had to leave the orphanage was getting close. Just when I believed that my life was about to end, God showed me how great He is.

He sent an amazing family and changed my life through them. To this day I am still amazed at His redeeming power. I truly believed to be a lost cause, but nobody is too far gone for Him to reach.

You have to go through the valley to reach a mountain. Today, all I want to do is to be in the valley to help others reach the top of a mountain. I want to be used by God.

Out of the Ashes

Nadia

My name is Nadia. I was born in Armenia. My father got married after I was born but not to my mother. When I was two months old, my mother took me to Moldova and I never knew my father. Two years later, my sister Silvia was born. My mother would often go to Russia for work to support our family so we grew up not having her around much. When I was eleven years old and Silvia was eight, we ended up in the largest orphanage in the country. I spent five awful years of unworthy existence there; everyday, I wondered what was going to come out of all this, how I would manage to be any different than all of the eight hundred kids around me, and how I would ever achieve something that would make me see myself worthy and make others proud of me. Just like every other child I dreamed of graduating from university and of doing something to leave good behind me in the world. But, dreaming in the orphanage was had because once you wake up, the cold, hard reality hits you in the face. At the time, I didn't know that there was a God watching over me so I made peace with the fact that there will be no success for me in life and that I was fine. Then, God sent someone to tell me otherwise. It was Philip Cameron – who is now my dad. At that time though, he was just a stranger who was giving me hope to hold on to so I wouldn't give up. I finally went to college and graduated with a degree in interior design; it was not easy but during those four years I got to know God and accept Him in my life. God worked perfectly during all the time that I was struggling, gave me a dad when I needed one, a home and a family. He healed me and finally proved to me that He created me perfectly, that I am His child, and that His child never fails.

Today I am a person who can truly say: "never walk alone in life because it will get you nowhere". All the courage, the confidence, the strength, the hope, the love, and the acceptance that I longed for, came from Him and Him alone. Over the years I achieved more then just a degree, more than I asked for and more than I wished for because God decided that I am worth more.

Dragalina
and Liliana

We were born in a family with eight children. We grew up in a cabin, in the forest, with no electricity. Our father was extremely abusive and strict on us. Our mother was always recovering from our father's constant beatings. One day our mother ran away and left all eight of us with our father. He was angry at our mother and let it out on us by forcing us to do hard labor. We remember the day when we saw our mother come back and we will never forget the happiness we felt – even though it was short lived. She was locked in the house and beaten so hard by our father we thought we would never see her alive again. We were all sitting outside and could hear her scream – begging for help. We were all crying and running around the house knocking on the windows, trying to get our father to stop beating the only person in the world who cared about us. That's all we could do at the moment; we were so helpless.

When we got older, we were sent to the orphanage. It was not the best place in the world, but it was honestly better than being at home with out father. And we didn't have to witness him beating our mother every day.

The teacher at the orphanage made jokes about our background and mocked us constantly because we had lived in the forest.

As graduation day at the orphanage grew closer, we were more and more worried about our future outside the orphanage. I (Liliana) remember wanting to disappear. Life did not make any sense, and I (Dragalina) did not want to go back to where I came from.

Just when we believed our life was about to get worse, God sent a family to us through whom He changed our life beyond our expectations. We are blessed and thankful to be part of the Cameron family and grateful to have Jesus in our heart.

Our heart is happy, our future is bright, and our God is great.

Out of the Ashes

Eugenia, Irina and Stefan

I am the second child in a family of four. Even though we lived in poverty I felt wealthy because I had a big family.

My world fell apart when I was eight years old when my father suddenly died of a heart attack. I still remember that late night kneeling around him with my brother and sisters crying and begging him not to leave us.

My father's death was the beginning of a difficult life. His death left us paralyzed with the fear of the unknown. My mother worked extremely hard to care for us. Four years later she died from kidney failure. Because I was left to care for her that day my auntie blamed me for her death.

My life had no meaning. It was filled with pain and suffering and I wanted to end it. After two months, I ran away from home and got hit by a car. I was in a coma for three days. I had no recollection of the accident and had a hard time remembering my family members. After they told me of what had happened I immediately regretted being alive. The pain of losing my parents was still tearing me apart and realizing that I was an inconvenience to my family made it even worse.

I was in constant pain because my right leg was injured extremely in the accident. I could not ask anyone for help as it was seen as a complaint and I was immediately reminded that I was a burden for my family.

My older sister was only thirteen years old when she promised my mother on her death that she would keep the family together no matter what. When our relatives tried to separate us and send us to an orphanage my sister begged them to let us live together. Life became about survival. My sister would go to work every day and I was left to care for our younger sister and brother at home. Some days I simply could not see beyond the pain I felt and the state of desperation that we were in. I tried to end my life countless times. I wanted the loneliness to end. I felt so defeated and saw life as being unfair to us. I was always wondering, "what did we do to deserve our parents taken away from us?"

When I turned sixteen, I went to the capital to continue my studies and that's where my life turned from a mess into a miracle.

One of my classmates was Natalia Sugar. Her kindness, sense of humor and positive view of life drew me to her and we became friends. During the summer, Sugar organized an outreach camp for friends from school.

Those few days during the camp have impacted my life immensely. I learned about Jesus and His unfailing love towards us. I realized that I was alive because He had a purpose for my life. Sugar's outreach program saved my life and the life of my family.

Shortly after the camp ended, I was introduced to the Cameron family who made the outreach program possible. The Cameron family has become my family since then. One of the many things they did for my family and I was to believe in us and see us worthy enough to give us a chance in life. Their love and support has built the foundation of what I want my life to be about.

God had reached out to me and my family through an outreach program organized by an orphan. Today, I wish for nothing more than to make that possible for others just like me. I want to become His hands through Orphans Hands.

Out of the Ashes

Galina
and Victor

My name is Galina. I am twenty-one years old. I was born in a very poor family with five siblings. We had to work hard every single day to afford food and clothing. My mother was always too busy with men to care for us. Her boyfriend at the time was very mean to us. He abused my mother and us daily. He kept all the food to himself and tried to starve us countless times. My mother was drunk most of the time. I still remember those days when we had to beg people in the village for food.

Because of the poverty we lived in we ended up in the orphanage. I was not accepted by the other kids at the orphanage. I was always rejected by them and I was never allowed to be part of their games. I felt so unwanted and I was always lonely. My mother never visited me. She had forgotten about my existence and that hurt me more than anything because it meant that the men in her life were more important than her children.

The day came when I had to leave the only place I called home. I was only sixteen-years-old. All I knew is that there was no place for me in the world. I was nothing but an orphan with nowhere to go and no one to care for me.

The day I met the Cameron family, I found out that God had a purpose for my life all along. Through them God rescued me and changed my life.

Out of the Ashes

Irina

My name is Irina. I was born in an alcoholic family. My mother had four children of four different fathers. I had a very difficult childhood; my parents were absent most of the time because they were drunk most days.

The only thing my father taught me is how to kill myself. I will never forget the late winter night when my father was beating my mother so hard that I thought he was going to kill her. I bit his leg to make him stop hurting her. My mother got away from him and took my older brothers and ran away with them leaving me alone with my drunken fathers. I was so afraid I could hardly breath. He grabbed me by the arm and threw me on the bed. He went away and came back with a razor blade. He handed it to me screaming, "I will teach you how to slit your wrists." "This is for your mother," he said. The next thing I remember is waking up in the hospital. I was hurt badly and spent the next month recovering in the hospital. I was alone and forgotten. I regretted not dying that night. One day my mother showed up and took me away. It was extremely cold outside and I kept asking her where she was taking me. We spent the next few days living on the streets and sleeping in abandoned elevators during the night.

My mother was drunk most of the time. One day we found an abandoned basement and we moved there to live with my brother. My older brother took on the responsibility to care for the family because my mother was absent most of the time.

Very soon my mother found a guy and she took us all to live with him. We spent a few years in his house. He was extremely abusive and was never happy about our presence there.

When I turned sixteen, I was given the chance to study in Moldova's capital city, Chisinau. One day a classmate invited me to church. That Sunday I met the Cameron family. I have never seen love and kindness like I saw through the Cameron family. Because of their heart to serve others and help the lost find their way I am who I am today. I am so thankful for the chance they gave me to change my life and not end up like my parents. I love Jesus and I know that without Him I am nothing. I want to share Him with all the lost souls out there. Orphans Hands gives hope and a hand to pick the fallen up.

Out of the Ashes

Galina

My name is Galina. I was abandoned by my parents when I was four-years-old and I have never heard from them since. I ended up in an orphanage and my life became a nightmare. The horrible conditions, broken roof, broken windows, no heating system, and a cold shower once a week, felt like nothing compared to the terrible condition my soul was in. I was hurt, broken, lonely and unloved. I became distant and did not trust anyone around me.

The nightmare ended on one December night. I was 14 years old and lost in a cruel world when I met the Cameron family. It was the night we celebrated Christmas at the orphanage and God sent hope in a dark corner of the world - my world. God shone a light over our orphanage through the Cameron's.

That night was the first time I was given a hug in my life, the first time I got a Christmas present, a birthday gift and my very first true smile.

It was difficult for me to understand why someone would sacrifice their time to come and spend time with a bunch of unwanted orphans. I got my answer when they first told me about God. He was the reason why. I consider that the most important gift I got from the Cameron family.

I have been part of the Cameron family for over fourteen years now. I learned that even though we are not blood related, they are the ones that accepted me when no one else knew of my existence. They are the ones that made a place for me in their life and have never given up on me since.

I am extremely thankful to God for everything He has given me. He lifted me up when I was bowed down in sorrow.

Today, I want to be used by God to help bring hope to those that are still in darkness and bring the gift of Jesus to all those that are bowed down in sorrow.

Out of the Ashes

Natalia

My name is Natalia, but everyone calls me Sugar. I have never been part of a real family. My father was an alcoholic who constantly abused my mother, my brother and I. My mother spent most of her time in the hospital recovering from the beatings she received. I never got the chance to spend time with her because of this. I will never forget the hopelessness I felt every time I saw my mother lying on the floor unconscious in a pool of blood.

I remember the countless times my father tried to kill me and my brother, and I'll never forget the cold, dark winter nights trying to escape his chasing after us with a knife.

When I was seven years old, the only family I knew fell apart and my world collapsed in front of me. My father died and shortly after his death I was abandoned by my mother at a bus station. She sat quietly next to my brother and I until the bus arrived. My brother took my hand and we made our way through the people rushing in and out of the bus. I turned my head and saw my mother through the back window of the bus, still standing outside waving goodbye. I cannot explain the desperation I felt in that moment. I felt as if every wall had closed in on me. I wanted to scream. I wanted to run. And, I wanted to cry. Instead, I sat there paralyzed with fear as the old yellow bus drove me further and further away from my mother. That was the last time I ever saw her.

I ended up in the orphanage at Ungheni, where I shared a painful existence with eight hundred other children. The conditions were bad and the food was only enough to keep us alive. The teachers never missed a chance to remind us of our shameful past and our empty future. We were mistakes made by our parents and unworthy of a future.

I had so much anger inside of me that soon I started to hate myself and everyone around me. I never allowed myself to dream because I saw myself worthless. The person that was supposed to love me unconditionally, my mother, rejected me. I gave up on myself and refused to see any value in me. I waited for nine years for my mother to come and visit me in the orphanage. She never did.

When I turned sixteen, I was put out of the orphanage, which had been my home for nine years. I was lost and I had nowhere to go. After living in different dormitories, moving from school to school, and struggling to survive on my own, I met the Cameron family.

My life was changed through the amazing work of this family. I was given a place to stay, a chance to continue studying, and most importantly, I was introduced to Jesus. I learned that God has an amazing plan for my life and that I am precious in His eyes.

In 2013, I graduated college with a major in Fashion Design and now I am studying Business and Administration. Being an orphan I was always at the risk of ending up being trafficked. I was given a chance in life because someone cared enough.

Today, I want to become His hands, through Orphans Hands I want to bring light into the darkest places and I want to tell the world about His unconditional love. This is my dream.

Out of the Ashes

Valentina

My name is Valentina. I was born in Ukraine to a very poor family. When I was only a year old my parents passed away and I was adopted by a family and taken to another country, Moldova.

My adoptive parents loved me very much. They were my entire world. When I was older a miracle happened and my mother (who thought she could have no children) got pregnant. She gave birth to my baby brother and we named him Andrei. My life was so full of joy and I was thankful to be part of the family and for the chance they had offered me in life.

Nine months later, I lost my adoptive father. He died from a heart attack. We became extremely poor after his death. My mother worked very hard to provide for my baby brother and me. I started skipping school in order to care for my brother while my mother worked. We barely survived. Five years later, my adoptive mother passed away as well. I was completely destroyed. I was not able to think and keep myself together. I felt as if I was falling into a deep hole from where I would never be able to get out. I had no hope. I could not understand what I had done to deserve the loss of two sets of parents. I sat and cried for days at the time because I felt so hopeless and so heart broken for my 5-year-old brother. I thought that God did not exist, and that if He did, He had forgotten about us. Today, I know that I was wrong.

One day a relative told me about the Cameron family and all the children in the same situation as me that they have helped. With a spark of hope in my heart I left for

Chisinau, the capital, to meet them and beg them for help. I left my younger brother in the care of my aunt and promised him that I would come back to him. Leaving him behind was one of the most difficult things I had to do in life, but I understood that his life depended on what I was about to do.

I went to Chisinau and showed up at the house that belonged to the Cameron family. Meeting them was one of the biggest blessings that God had given me. They immediately accepted me like their own and have loved me from the first moment they met me. Through them, God has shown me that He has not forgotten about me, that He loves me unconditionally, and that He has a purpose for my life.

Recently I graduated from university with a major in Fashion Design. I am able to help my little brother and give him hope for a better life.

My wish is to be a part of God's vision, to bring people out of darkness to bring healing to the broken hearted through His word and love.

Orphans Hands is the vision that offers a better life in Him to the unloved and the unwanted.

Nicoleta

My name is Nicoleta. At the age of five I was abandoned by my mother left to live with my father. Even though he was disabled, he cared for me and my little sister for a year. The day my mother returned I hoped for a better life and a happy family. Instead my sister and I were taken away from our father to live with our grandparents. It felt as if I was nothing but a stranger to them and an unwanted burden. I spent most of my days there locked in a room with my sister, day and night. My grandmother would leave a few pieces of bread and water - just enough for us to survive on. One day my mother showed up again and

I was so happy to see her. I hoped that she would take us away. My heart broke when by mistake I overheard my mother's conversation with my grandmother. They were discussing plans to sell me and my sister. I can't even begin to explain what I felt as I listened. The people that are supposed to have unconditional love were planning how to get rid of my little sister and me! I lost the the little hope I had and felt so unwanted and rejected.

Somehow my auntie found out about their plan. We were taken back to live with our father. Unfortunately, that did not last long. He was not able to work and provide for us due to his disabled condition. My father sent my sister and me to the largest orphanage in the country.

I spent nine years at the orphanage and they were the worst nine years of my life. The teachers treated us like we weren't humans.

When I turned sixteen, I left the orphanage. I had nowhere to go and no one to care for me until I met an amazing family. God had a plan all along. He was watching over me all those years that I lived in hurt and darkness. God changed my life through the amazing Cameron family.

Out of the Ashes

Angela

My name is Angela. A few years after I was born my parents lost their home and we all ended up on the street. My grandmother felt sorry for us and took us in. There were ten people living in a two-bedroom apartment. The apartment had no heating and no water. It was extremely cold during the winter. My parents did not have a job and we barely stayed alive due to lack of food.

One day my parents realized that there was no way they could care for me. I ended up at one of the largest orphanages in Moldova. I was only five years old. The teachers were never nice to me or the other kids. Every

Christmas the teachers would take away the gifts that people from America would send to us and give them to their own children.

I missed my parents and I wanted to be with them. Every chance I got to see them I begged them to take me away with them. I felt like I was just a number, that no one knew my name. I spent eleven years in the orphanage.

When I turned sixteen, I had to leave the orphanage. I had no where to go and no one to help me. I felt more hopeless than I felt in the orphanage. One day I heard about an amazing family, the Camerons, who built homes and gave hope to kids like me. I went and met the Cameron family, and my life has changed completely since then.

The opportunity they gave me, gave me a spark of hope for my future. They have accepted me, loved me and believed in me. I now have hope, and my dream is to let God use me to bring hope to other lost souls like I once was. Orphans Hands is not just a spark of hope for me, but for all the hopeless people out there.

Out of the Ashes

Maria

My name is Maria. I spent ten years in the largest orphanage in Moldova. My parents made this decision because they believed it was the best choice they could make for me. My mother was ill and spent most of her time in a hospital bed. My father worked in construction and never had a stable job. We were in a constant struggle to survive.

I never liked the orphanage. I was another lost child, another failure that added to the statistics. Time went by and before I knew it I was sixteen-years old and about to end up on the street. All I knew at the time was that I was not ready to face the world on my own. I was not ready to leave the place that I had called my home for the last ten years. What I did not know was that God had it all figured out. He knew of my existence and had an amazing plan for my life. Through the Cameron family, He saved my life.

Out of the Ashes

Tatiana

My name is Tatiana. I grew up in a very poor family in Moldova. My father never accepted me as his daughter and my mother always viewed my older sister and me as a poor inconvenience in her life. Until I turned eleven-years-old I lived with my mother and my sister in the village. My mom had a boyfriend who hated my sister and me. He was my mother's priority in life during the eight years that they lived together and he always made sure that she knew we were not welcome in his world. He was extremely cruel towards us. One day he tried to rape my sister and she ran away from home. As always, my mother saw this as being our fault and said that my sister and I were the biggest two mistakes she had made in life and that we were nothing but two obstacles that complicated her relationship with her boyfriend.

Just when I thought life could not get any worse, my mother was taken to prison. She worked at the village grocery store and had huge debt because she allowed people to get food on credit. Because they couldn't pay in time, my mother was held accountable for all the money. She was given six-and-a-half years in prison. I was only ten years old when the only family I had was taken away from me. Shortly afterward, I was sent to the orphanage because I had no one to care for me.

One of the most painful things that I had to overcome when I got to the orphanage was to let my mother go and to accept the idea that I might never get to see her again. For ten years she was all I had and I longed for her every single day I spent in the orphanage.

For six years the orphanage became my home. I made friends and I had my older sister with me. I was happy. I had a bed to sleep in, enough food to keep me from starving, and I was safe from my mother's boyfriend.

One thing I was not safe from was the cruel words of the teachers that have haunted me all these years. No matter how hard I tried I was never good enough for them. Most of them physically abused us every chance they got just to prove that they were superior.

At sixteen years of age I, like all the kids, was put out of the orphanage and had to find a way to face life and survive on my own. I had no hope in life. I felt lost and defeated by all the hardships. The day I thought my world was ending I met the Cameron Family. They provided a home for me, gave me a chance to get an education and have shown me God's love. God had chosen them to be the ones through whom He worked in my life. I would not be who I am today if it was not for the people that cared and invested in my life.

My wish today is to help the ones left behind just like I once was. Through Orphans Hands I want to tell them that there is hope and there is a Heavenly Father that loves them unconditionally.

Out of the Ashes

Ulizana

My name is Ulizana. My mother was born into a wealthy family in Moldova. Because of this she got the opportunity to go and study medicine in Russia. There, she met my father, a citizen of Kyrgyzstan and they got married. My mother gave birth to my three older sisters before she discovered that the man she married was extremely cruel. He physically abused her every chance he got. Her life became a nightmare and she became afraid for the lives of my sisters. When she found out that she was pregnant with me she decided to run away. My mother and sisters returned to Moldova where I was born.

The physical abuse had affected her immensely; she became mentally ill and was not able to care for my sisters and me any longer. I was abandoned as a baby at a tuberculosis hospital and my older sisters were put into an orphanage.

I spent the first ten years of my life in the hospital. I didn't know my real name; they called me Cristina. I knew nothing about my family or why I ended up there. For ten years I received the tuberculosis treatment even though I was not sick. I had so much hate towards that place. The doctors were always mean to me because I looked different. My Asian appearance gave the other children a reason to constantly make fun of me.

I spent so many nights dreaming that one day I would be part of a family. Every day I watched the other children as their parents visited them. I had no visitors for ten years.

When I turned ten-years-old, I met a very strange woman. She showed up one day at the hospital and introduced herself as my mother and told me that I had three older sisters.

I cannot explain the hope I felt in my heart when I met her. I was taken out of the hospital and transferred to the same orphanage where my sisters had spent the last ten years. Meeting my sisters was one of the happiest moments in my life. We all cherish the feeling of belonging and at ten years old, I felt that I "belonged" for the first time in my life.

Unfortunately, my joy did not last long. My sisters told me that our mother was mentally ill. They advised me to stay away from her when she came to visit because she was dangerous. Realizing that I gained and lost the most precious thing in a child's life in one day broke my heart and left me even more disappointed than before. Loneliness and desperation took over my being and I refused to let anyone into my heart being afraid of getting hurt again.

When I was fifteen years old I had to leave the orphanage. I had nowhere to go because the only homes I'd had for past fifteen years were the tuberculosis hospital and the orphanage.

During that summer, I went to a Christian camp where I heard about Jesus. I remember praying so much that He would give me a home and watch over me when I had to face the world on my own. A few months later I was introduced to the Cameron family and every dream I had as an orphan became a reality. God has truly blessed me with a family and has watched over me every step of the way. I often ask myself how come I am so blessed; why do I have this life when I see so many people that still struggle. I don't want to say that I am unthankful, but I am concerned about others. It is hard for me to know that people like me, having a soul like me, sharing the same desires to be loved and to love, seeking peace like me, are suffering so much and are full of sorrows and disappointments. We all have the power to change the world, and that is what I want to do.

Orphans Hands is God's miracle for every orphan, a spark of hope for the lost and a touch of love for the ones in need.

Out of the Ashes

Iuliana

My name is Iuliana. I am seventeen years old. I was born into an alcoholic family. I do not remember my parents ever being sober. When I was little, I got sick and with time, I lost my ability to hear. My older brother and I spent most of our time on the streets of the city begging for food. My parents never acknowledged the fact that they had two children to care for. Every single day they chose alcohol over us. When I turned four, I was sent to live at the deaf kindergarten. This did not replace the need I had for a family but at least I was fed daily and I had a place to sleep. During vacations, my brother and I were sent to the village so our grandparents could care for us. Instead of loving us they threw us back out on the street. The good thing is, I never heard any of those angry words that my grandma was screaming at us while throwing us out of her house.

When I was seven years old while at the deaf and mute orphanage, one of my classmates and I were stolen and taken away by a man. We were taken to this man's house and threatened with an axe if we made a wrong move. He locked us in his house with no food and no water. I just remember looking at the axe and being so afraid. One day he forgot to lock the door and I ran outside. We were rescued after the police put the man in custody and we were returned to the orphanage. At sixteen years of age I graduated from the orphanage and I found myself on the street once again. My father remarried and his wife wanted nothing to do with me. They did not even allow me to enter their home. My mother was living on the street and was always drunk. The government gives twenty dollars monthly to help people like me. Unfortunately, I never saw the money. My mother spent everything she got on alcohol. Until one week ago, I had no future, no family and no hope. I am so thankful to Orphans Hands for giving me a home and a family. For the very first time in my life I had the chance to eat at the table with a family. Thank you Orphans Hands for making space for me at the table of hope. God had answered my prayers. He truly is amazing.

Out of the Ashes

Irina

My name is Irina. I am 18 years old. I was born in Ukraine in a family where both of my parents where alcoholics and drug addicts. We were extremely poor and my parents wanting nothing to do with me and my sister. My sister and I spent most of our time on the street - hungry.

When I was four years old, my drunken father burned me with a torch while torching the pig. I remember being on fire. I was taken to the hospital and barely survived. Half of my body and face was burnt. When I turned seven years old, my auntie felt sorry for me and took me away from my alcoholic parents. I moved with her to Moldova. Not long afterward I was sent to the deaf and mute orphanage in Cahul where I stayed until I turned sixteen.

I never had a real family. I never knew how it felt to belong and to be loved. I felt like an obstacle for everyone.

The happiest moment in my life was when I got a phone call from Orphans Hands and they offered me a home, a family, and a chance for a better future. My dream is to become a massage therapist. I am so thankful for the beautiful home, for the food on the table and for everyone who cared enough to make this life possible for me. I now have hope. I love you guys, even though I never met you.

Liuda

My name is Liuda. I am 19 years old. When I was still a child my parents got divorced. My mother, my older brother and I we went to live with my step-father. Because I was deaf I was put in the orphanage. When I was seven years old, my entire family was murdered by burglars -my mother, my step-father, my older brother, and my baby brother. They also set the house on fire to get rid of the evidence. When I heard about what had happened I could not stop crying and they called an ambulance for me. Every single night, I used to dream that we were together and that everything was fine. When I awoke in the morning, my world became filled with darkness again. Being deaf and in the orphanage is what saved me from the destiny they had. I was left in the care of my uncle who had five children of his own. Neither him or his family spoke to me because they never learned how to sign. I was always so lonely because of this.

I spent nine years in the orphanage. Very soon the orphanage became the only family I had. Not a single day went by when I did not miss my family and when I did not wonder how it would feel to have them alive. I have longed for a family for so long. When I was given the chance to be a part of a God-sent family, the Orphans Hands family, I could not believe it. My dream is to learn to read and write and become a hair stylist.

I love God with all I am. He has had a plan all along. I am so thankful for the opportunity to have a family where I know no loneliness, no pain, no hate. Thank you Orphans Hands and all who made my life possible.

Out of the Ashes

Maria

My name is Maria. I am twenty-one years old. I was born prematurely and after six months of treatments, I lost my hearing. My parents did not care about me. I do not remember once seeing them sober. Alcohol was the most important thing to my parents. We lived a miserable life. My father physically abused my mother and us constantly. I tried countless times to commit suicide because I did not see life worth living. I was saved by my auntie after trying to hang myself. My life was a nightmare. Verbal and physical abuse was always present and the smell of alcohol suffocated me.

Out of the Ashes

Once I was sent to the deaf and mute orphanage things got a little better. It was my place of escape, where I tried my best to forget my alcoholic parents. Unfortunately, two years ago I graduated and I had to return back to my parents and the miserable life with no future.

I was so lost, so desperate for a different kind of life than what my parents had to offer me. I was so tired of the darkness they were living in and the hopelessness that surrounded me.

The day that I was contacted by Orphans Hands was the day I learned what hope looks like. I did not want to remain for another day in my parent's home and left immediately. I was offered a home, a safe place where I can dream and hope, where I feel that I belong. I feel so loved by God. He has not forgotten me.

I am thankful to all of you who showed me what hope is and gave me the chance to dream and become someone in life. I cannot believe the opportunity I have been given. God is amazing.

Cristina

My name is Cristina. I was born into a family with five children. When I was only a few months old, I became seriously ill and lost my hearing. When I was little, my older and younger brother died. My family has never managed to overcome the loss. My parents could not deal with the loss and they turned to alcohol, trying to drown their sorrow in it. Very soon they started to neglect the rest of us. At the age of three, I was put into the orphanage for deaf children. My parents did not visit me for three years. I was too young to understand what was happening, but I was not too young to feel forgotten and alone. My family was terribly poor and could never afford to care for me. They never had the means to clothe me and I always wore used clothes that other people provided for me. During holidays I was sent home from the orphanage; even though I was surrounded by family members, I lived in total silence and loneliness. My family never communicated with me because they never cared enough to learn sign language. At times, I felt so unwanted - just another obstacle thrown into my family's life, another addition to the miserable life they already had. I spent most of my time at the orphanage believing and trying to accept that my destiny was set and that's how it was supposed to go. My life got worse when I aged out of the orphanage system and soon realized that I had no future. Those who are deaf like me are nothing but a burden in our society; everyone looks down at us.

I decided to go to a vocational school for the deaf to become a seamstress; I wanted to be able to earn enough money to survive on. A few months ago my roommate was raped and I became very afraid to sleep at night in the school dormitory. One day, one of my classmates told me about The Orphan's Hands - an organization like no other in my country – and it gave me hope. I could not believe what she told me until the night I sat down at the dinner table with my new family. There is truly a light at the end of the tunnel. I am so thankful for the safe home and the chance for a better future. I want to extend my deep gratitude to everyone who saw us worthy enough to be rescued and worthy enough to be given a chance in life.

Out of the Ashes

Maria

My name is Maria. My parents had four children – including one set of twins. I am one of the twins. I was weaker than my twin brother and was born undeveloped. The doctors told my mother that that was the reason I was born deaf. My parents got divorced when I was eleven years old and my father became an alcoholic. To this day he lives alone and I have never seen him sober. At two years of age, I was put into the orphanage and I was only visited a couple of times over the course of the next fourteen years. My mother explained to me that the reason she could not visit me was because she had to save money to care for my brothers and sister. I spent most of my holidays at the orphanage alone because no one cared enough to come and take me home.

I made myself believe that no one wanted a deaf child - a thought that was extremely painful to accept. My world was completely silent and lonely, my heart had no hope, and my life had no future. Once I aged out of the orphanage system at only sixteen years of age, I went on to learn to become a seamstress at the only vocational deaf school in my country. I was not ready to face the outside world but it was the only choice I had in order to survive. I was afraid because in my country, no one employs deaf girls like me. We are ignored and pushed aside by those around us.

When I was given the chance to become part of The Orphans Hands my life became like a dream. I am given a home just like in movies. I am amazed at how much my life has changed, amazed at the amazing people I now get to call my family, and amazed at the chance of being truly happy.

Out of the Ashes

Radu

My name is Radu. I was blessed to be born into a family where I was loved by my parents. I had a beautiful life with my parents until I turned six-years-old when my parents started to argue more and more about money. In order to survive, my father left to work abroad leaving my mother and me in Moldova. As soon as he found a job in Russia he made sure that my mother and I were well taken care of. We were doing alright materially speaking, but I missed my father and wanted him back. One day my mother got a phone call that changed our life forever. My father lost his life in a car accident. I have never been the same since. I remember how hard it was for my mother to keep going. Not only were we still mourning my father, we were struggling financially. Witnessing our struggle, my aunt advised my mother to send me to the orphanage where I would be taken care of and educated. My mother was against the idea at first but once she realized that she had no other choice, she accepted it. I spent nine years at the orphanage. It was cold during the winters. We were only fed enough to be kept alive, allowed to take one shower a week, and were surrounded by a bunch of teachers who never saw us as human beings.

At sixteen years of age I graduated. I was afraid to face the future on my own and did not know what to do with my life. Through a friend, I met the Cameron family and I was given the most amazing opportunity in my life: the chance to have a family, to continue my education, and to change my future for the better. I am so thankful for everyone that cared enough and saw me worthy enough to invest in my life, and for telling me about Jesus. My dream is to bring hope to others that are in the same desperate situation as I was a few years ago.

Out of the Ashes

Sergiu

My name is Sergiu. I was born in a loving and caring family but that did not last for long. One day my father found out that he was very sick and needed urgent treatment. My parents sold everything they owned in order to pay for the expensive treatment. My father never recovered and died not long after. I was eight years old and my older sister was twelve when we were abandoned by our mother. She went abroad to find work in order to provide for us. We were left in the care of our relatives. When my mother realized that she could not provide for us anymore she sent us to the orphanage. She did not visit us much. One of the hardest things we had to overcome when we entered the orphanage is that life would never be the same again. We felt so unwanted and so unloved. Every single day, the teachers would tell that we were not worthy and that we did not matter to anyone. As time went by, their words became more real and I was not able to get them out of my head. I became so hopeless and so defeated in my soul. After spending eight years in the orphanage my time was coming to an end. I had nowhere to go and no one to help me. Just when I thought that my life was coming to an end God showed me that He had a different plan. Through my sister, I was introduced to the Cameron family and the work they were doing for the orphans of Moldova. They gave me a chance to a better life. They have inspired me by believing in me. Their love has given me hope. I was amazed at how God had turned things around for the better. With the Cameron's help I graduated High School and I am not about to start my sophomore year in university to become an interior designer. Today I know that I belong to God and I am His child. Through Orphans Hands I am given the chance to make His name and love known. Thank you.

How You Can Help

Make a donation. Please give a gift today at **www.theorphanshands.org/donate**

Pray for our ministry. Please pray for us as we pray for you.

Start a gift drive. We are always in need of new coats, boots, toys, nonperishable food items, and much more.

Take a mission trip. Change a life while you change your own! Visit Moldova and spend your days ministering to young men and women who have grown up being told they were worthless.

Share this book with your friends and family. Share these stories of redemption with your friends and family and help us tell our story.

Invite The Orphans Hands to come and share at your church. We have a team of young men and women from Moldova travelling in the States for most of the year. We would love to share our stories with your organization. To schedule us, send us an email at **contact@theorphanshands.org**